# PREFACE FOR LEAVING HOMELAND

## SALAWU OLAJIDE

Published by Akashic Books
©2019 Salawu Olajide

ISBN: 978-1-61775-748-8



Akashic Books
Brooklyn, New York, USA
Ballydehob, Co. Cork, Ireland
Twitter: @AkashicBooks
Facebook: AkashicBooks
E-mail: info@akashicbooks.com
Website: www.akashicbooks.com

African Poetry Book Fund
*Prairie Schooner*
University of Nebraska
110 Andrews Hall
Lincoln, Nebraska 68588

# TABLE OF CONTENTS

To say these poems are timely would be accurate, but they are also timeless. The subject the poet gives shape and voice to in *Preface to Leaving Home-land* is the physical, political, and psychological condition of those who are forced to leave their homeland or whose homeland renders them stateless within its borders. The past two decades of migration of Africans seeking asylum in Europe is the primary site of Salawu Olajide's engagement with a longstanding moral question: what is the cost of turning from those need-ing refuge?

Several of the poems in the collection recast or allude to present events, drawing upon reports by journalists who have been documenting the humanitarian crisis taking place at the modern day nexus of Africa and Europe—the "New Middle Passage," as the Mediterranean crossing has been called in recent years. That naming, as with Olajide's poems, directs attention to how racism and Europe's centuries-long history of slavery and colonization play an oversized role in the treatment of African migrants.

Lampedusa is one of the geographic locales on the route of Africans trying to reach Europe and it appears again and again in Olajide's poems for good reason. In the past two decades, over 400,000 migrants/refugees from Libya, Somalia, Eritrea, and several other African nations, as well as from Syria, have undertaken the dangerous journey overland, then via sea, to reach this small Italian island near Sicily. In 2013, Lampedusa was the location of one of the most tragic of these crossings when a ship carrying 518 asylum seekers sank half a mile off its coast. 366 of the passengers on-board drowned. Images of that particular shipwreck and of the dessert and sea—of dunes, mirages, waves, sharks, the "broken wooden boat"—return and return, haunting the poems.

Despite Olajide's evocation of this and other connected events and his artful echoing of the past, these are not documentary, nor solely historical, nor truly even narrative poems. They work not so much through the force of the story—the contours of which are quickly sketched or alluded to briefly in a title, epigraph, or image—as they do through the power of the lyric. These are dirges, lamentations, and prayers. Olajide uses anaphora, refrain, and rhetorical and syntactical repetition to create a plangent, intimate voice of witness.

Frequently in this collection Olajide assumes the voice of real individuals who survived the Mediterranean passage. In "Lampedusa, through the Eyes of Fanus," for example, he enters the perspective of one of the five women who survived (out of eighty women aboard) the shipwreck in 2013 off Lampedusa and who was briefly profiled in a *Guardian* article that followed. In his poem, the poet places us inside Fanus's mind, granting access to her virtually unimaginable hours spent in the water, wondering whether she would drown, be taken by sharks, or be "welcomed" by those on shore, that "light dimming faraway."

While I greatly admire the work of journalists, the problem with how we read news is that we often quickly forget, perhaps seek to forget, the suffering of the individual or individuals embedded in the account of what happened. By bringing the consciousness of migrants into focus, in language that is both distilled and incantatory, Olajide's poems do not allow us to move past the visceral experiences of others so easily. In that sense, his poems are also about memory.

In "Hakim Bellow Writes Letter Home," Olajide inhabits the voice of Bello, a Nigerian who migrated to Berlin via Libya and Lampedusa. The poem, an imagined "letter home," expresses an essential tension: between the desire those back home have to imagine the family member or lover or friend who survives the journey to be in a "cozy" life versus the actual life for many African migrants once they land in Europe. Even those granted asylum often experience great difficulty, both in practical terms (finding employment, housing, etc.) and in psychological ones. Bello's "memories"— the "scenes of the sea" he tries to put behind him and of "weeding [a] path to freedom"—are notably interposed throughout the letter, evoking the trauma survivor's difficult negotiation between the present and the past.

There are a couple poems in the collection not centred on migration, which return to an earlier period of African history: apartheid in South Africa. In one of these poems, Olajide alludes to the famous photograph taken at the start of the Soweto uprisings of 1976—a photograph that was circulated in newspapers around the world and is credited as playing a crucial role in helping to bring about apartheid's end. In placing Salawu Olajide's spare, incadescent poems alongside that photograph, I think again of the power of such art: to remind us to remember, to teach us how to see, and to give us the space to feel.

# VACANCY FOR AN ASYLUM SEEKER

they say:
stop looking for
what you cannot find in a land that calls you stranger

they say:
do not refuse what this land
offers you,  and accept the gift like God's offering

they say:
you have no previous background in this land
you visit through Europe's backdoor

they say:
you do not carry the vocabularies
this city wants,  and your body smells of the desert

they ask:
how many years you have spent in this land?
they ask, "how may we help you?"

# GOODBYE TO LAMPEDUSA

It is what they say
because the sea does not have footprints
to see where others have ended their journeys,
and today—this incandescent afternoon—
they tell you to follow
the path of the wind,
follow it to where the water leads you
as a new merchandise arrives
with a parcel of goodbye.

Goodbye is what they tell you
as your final parting gift, so close
your heart to unholy thoughts
about the waves.

# DEAR LAMPEDUSA

I would like to say
I would come back to you

I would like to say I would not come
back: body-mangled and tags around necks

I would like to say I would return
to pay homage to the white bone of memories at your seabed

I would like to say I shall return
as a tourist watching your waters and their flowers

I would like to say
I shall never come riding in this broken wooden boat again

# HAKIM BELLO WRITES LETTER HOME

You think about me
that now, I am
in a cosy sofa in one
European city under their neon lights
listening to Cardi B's Bodak Yellow
and eroding my odd memories
putting all the scenes of the seas behind me.

You think about me
sitting on a bench by a boulevard
watching my dreams grow
like flower pollinated by the motionless sun,
its scent spreading toward
where the city begins.

You think about me in a Beoing 707
floating midair peeping through the window,
breaking my body against the clouds,
flying back home with a golden beak.
You never think I am in Agadez
weeding my path to freedom.

# DUNE

The dune will lead you to the heart
of the desert, where humans' bodies litter
the earth like rags. The dune
will hum to you how many lives
are buried beneath this fine brown sand
and how many are coming to be buried. The dune
will tell you how to embrace dust
and break your body within it. The dune
will whisper to you the raider's stories.
The dune will teach you how to drink
urine as an oasis for your thirst.
The dune will teach you how to appreciate trees
and their shed of love.
The dune will bring back
the face of your mother on the mirage
calling for your body to return home.

# LAMPEDUSA, THROUGH THE EYES OF FANUS

(Fanus says)

*"I'd never been in a body of water before. I was trying to stay afloat by splashing
my hands like a dog."*

The water says run and the waves say so too,
my body hangs on proving courage to the shards of metal
carrying us from the bank of Libya
but now sinking.

How do you run on water when your hands are not fins
and everyone is holding on to the other struggling
to stay afloat this undulating surface? How do you swim
when the metallic hope cracks at the bottom and gives you out
to the sea in the dead of the night? How do you hold to floating
bodies half-eaten by sharks? How do you know that the light dimming faraway
is waiting to welcome you?

# RETRIEVAL

This is the part where the sea-rejects
return as dead bodies rolling on water
and divers drag them to the shores.

This is the part you should never
mention to your mother when
you set to dare the face of the ocean.

This is the part where two dead lovers
hug each other
and their spirits float on water as flotillas.

This is the part where they take your body
to an unmarked grave
and sing the requiem for eyeless sockets.

This is the part where you do not end
up in the mouth of shark; this is the part
where you are dead and your wife is as well.

# AN IMMIGRANT'S COMPLAINT

I try to grow my own tree in Soweto
and pull a throne for myself out of the wood,
out of this earth. I try to see
the rainbow-less April
when Sithole's body
lay withered like a flower.

They say, goodbye, go back to your home.
But here, my tree grows,
the fruits blossom,
the flowers feed on the sun,
the cricket hops
without fear of being trapped in the darkness
of Grahamstown:
where you imagine all strangers without pants
uprooted like foreign hibiscuses.

I try to grow my own tree in Soweto
beyond this hurricane raging on my skin.

# WHAT GREETS YOU WHEN YOU GET HOME

What greets you when you get home; the trees greet you blistering.
The path you left has expanded its stomach and it no longer
admits feet alone. Machines have rented the street.
Your arrival marks the third anniversary of your father's lung disease.
Your father sits at the side of an aspen tree while the wind breaks on his naked
body waiting one day for you to return. He sits there
on the bamboo chair until the sun goes down.
At the open veranda lies your mother's grave which has grown some
odd flowers to her memories. Your old friend has turned the village priest;
he already predicts your coming. At your arrival, children gather around you
like a modern god. They shout a name you no longer hear.

What greets you when get home: Are you embraced by mud-wall? Or,
welcomed by a cow dung cemented floor? Your ears have lost the lyrics
    maidens sing
when they see virile men. You break and turn as one approaches you;
shrug her off. In the distance the wave of the city reaches your ears
stifling your yearning. What greets you when you get here?
Your brother greets you; you no longer hear
your father speak in old proverbs that sound odd.
Your sister is now married with children; you might never see her again.
What greets you when you get home?
Your eyes look for rediscovery in between the crevice
opposite the red-mud wall.

# PRAYER FOR AN ASYLUM SEEKER

May you find home
in the mouth of this shark
longing for your blood
and haunting your dreams.

May this darkness receive you
as part of its body  and protect
you from the phalanges; may you
find light at the end of this road.

May there be an oasis in this desert
when you get there; may your body
become the wind when the storm
rises like mountains rolling you homeward.

May this land wean you
as part of its own; may you never
be turned into a beast
you are never before.

## KANAKO*

Yesterday, I found myself at the end
of the journey I started a day before.
I was entering Sicily with an Eritrean boy
who drank his mother's blood and gave her
a funeral where sun was the only mourner
tearing through our skins. We, among other
ghoulish faces, face iron-bar fences
while our lips are rented with grief
and our eyes are too dehydrated to pool an ocean.

Father told me this is what happens
when we dream. Father told me
our bodies become birds levitating
through the air. Father told me
everybody carries a strange city in their body.
Father said it is where we go when we submit
to the heaviness of the eyes. Father told me
Kanako only turns your road into a dream of mirage.

*Kanako's is a mystical power in Yoruba belief that helps
reduce the length of a road.*

# AFTER YOU LEFT

Your mother becomes a pillar of grief
and the follicles of her body
become the holes where cactuses grow.
Two years before,
your sister left on the same path,
and banished herself into an eternity
of silence.

After you left, the family portrait becomes
your mother's company. In it, you are wearing
a red gown and a purple smile standing by the side of
your brother who died before the city
said, "Go, your body does not belong here." Your father,
with his wide grin, sitting on a king-size chair,
stares into the future beyond the shutters.

Your mother offers her body to the wind,
searching for your face in towns
where geography is learnt by the patterns on
the palms. After you left, your mother plants a flower
in your memory,  hoping the sun
will connect the plant and your body.

## "QOLORHA-BY-THE-SEA"

*After Zakes Mda*

Like the ocean, you bring so many things back to me.
I am ready to travel on you.
I shall sail in through the torrent
of your body. And when I arrive,
like a stranger with red ochre
in your heart of redness
which Mda says is beautiful home of civilization,
the wind of your heart shall carry me
through your ventricles.
So,
shall I sit on your capillaries
and fill myself with memories of unlit rooms
where our teeth are halogens?
Shall I perch on your veins
and imagine that each of your eyes
is a sun? Or, move into your artery
and tell the story where love begins with purple flower?

# OBSERVATORY NOTES FOR REFUGEE LOOKING FOR LOVE

You are looking
for love in the hearts of women in this city
where men hunt for passion and desire is
written with hieroglyphs of fear
to avoid expulsion by night.

A lady winks
at you to come near her naked
body, she says, "Let me give you life;
let me give you hope." Your heart turns turbulent
again like the waves at the bank of Lampedusa.

Love becomes an albatross
hanging around your neck
and you, an ornithologist, keep
looking for a nest in which
your body will become a residence.

You remember your wife
resting on your bosoms,
her fingers moving through the geography
of your body, her mouth a threshold of jeremiads
for your absence.

# NOTES TO THE ERITREAN BOY WHO MAY NEVER SEE HIS FATHER AGAIN

(let this poem accompany you)

Say goodbye to your father
you may never see again
taken by this land he thinks
will clothe your body
from the surging cold hand of winter
and fury of wind that follows
you from your home.

Say goodbye, as these unkind hands
tear you apart and talons
of strange men grope around your body.
Say goodbye,
as they lead you into the black orbit
of this city's darkness alone.

Never walk this path again
to find the missing body of your father.
Follow the road to Cayuga
where other children are
looking for eyes that care
in this land where hopes are strewn
on the street like carcasses.

# LAST NIGHT IN BARKIN LADI

The town says, "Leave. Leave now."
Its voice once full of people, now perforated,
and smoke burning over its head
and wanton souls of women escaping
in the fog of darkness.

*Leave. Leave now.*
I linger on a bit, listening to the infinite chaos
of the bird cries, and the charred body
of a small boy held by a headless bosom of a
mother on a cold, blood-stained plateau.

Today, I become the poet of shadow again
walking with bare soles in this darkling
damask with terror-ache of desire
following my feet where they may lead me
out of this jungle-heated touch of my land
where men are grazed on. Tell me
travellers, where it is not burning
in this country.

# ACKNOWLEDGMENT

With grateful acknowledgment to the *New Orleans Review* for providing a platform for me to publish "What Greets You When You Get Home," a poem included in this collection.